Papers on my floor

T'challa Williams

Books may be purchased in quantity and/or special sales by contacting the publisher, T'challa Publications, at 16 East Morningside Street, Hartford, Connecticut 06112 or by email tnwpublications@gmail.com.

Williams, T'challa, 1974 – Papers on my floor

ISBN-13: 978-0692408179

ISBN-10: 0692408177

Poetry

First Edition

Printed in United States

Cover photograph by Richard K. Williams

Dedicated to every artist that ever dared to put pen to page.......write on family....Right on!

T'challa

Papers on my floor

Contents of my papers...

<u>SPRING</u>

I Sing

<u>SUMMER</u>

Red Clay
The Resilient
Progeny
Fair Trade
Clemency
Shout out to the Mothers
The Moral of the ...Really?
Bae
Closed for Cleansing
Stout
Slow Down
Say no more
This Love
I'm Smitten
Nothing
Link Up
Say what now?
R & R
Until
To Die For
Drifting
Answering Machine
Just Say No
Blissfull Kisses
Seated
Ebony Sunrise
Oh
Alignment
Untitled

Fingertips

Harmony

Wedding Band

Observe

Love

On

Flix

The Color of my flowers

Intimacy

FALL

Seasonal

Morning

Beat

Why we eat so much bullshit?

righteous

Up the Road

Terminated

The Start of it All

Prisoner of war

Mountains

History

The Gift

Little One

On my Terms

You Don't Own Me

Silence

Manual Constraint

Speaking to the Goddess

Theorizing pontificates

Wait...What?

Shedding of the fallacy

Bye
Damn!
Thinking of You
Pen & No Paper
Love Fucking Hurts
Just Grow!
Scratch & Smoke Blues
Scattered
Random
On Locing up
Open the door (to the 9)
You don't wanna war with us
Big bones & undertones
Fragrance
Love's Respite
Discharged
Dead Seeds
Falling
Last Man
Transitional
A Changing of the Guard
You Must Learn
Losing
We Good
Fighting the fall
Before Anyone Else

Spring

Can you?

Labored breathing
In
Out
Steady rocking
Pausing to see
Can heart rate be slowed down
Nothing is working
Hot flash & slow pulsating veins
Blood rushing to improper locations
Uncompensated vocations
Swollen peaks
Leaks

Breathe
Rock
Stop

I cannot
Control
Desire

Coming

It is less of a coming
More of a stepping into
A return to a specific consciousness
A familiarity with an over-standing of
What it took
To make you who you are

Sankofa

Confidence and knowing returns in rare form
I could maneuver my way with eyes closed
Following the scent of my history
Through blocks, buildings, dialects, and
Remnants of childhood
Nostalgia over buildings that once housed
Lessons learned
Turns into blank stares at empty lots
What once was, is now not
Heartbeat strong
There is nothing like
Coming home

Loving my people

Black People
Do you know I love you
Stayed and prayed
Tried and true
Loving you for you

I am loving ups
Loving downs
Are you loving yourself
Because I am seeing frowns
Dreams being put down
So you can exist
On your current playing ground
But life contains hills
And if you stay in the valley
Avalanches will kill
However from the mountain top
Avalanches are ways to
Make the bullshit drop

Stop

My meditation always works
For the wrong things
It's amazing what your body will ensure you
Line up
Sign up
Come up on and keep going strong
But when you need to use your powers
For good
Delayed, they are
Estranged
Choked out by children of a lesser god

In response

How could I not get excited
about that
beautiful chocolate skin
Wrapped in pink and black lace
Wearing joy upon face
Sun kissed complexion
That beautiful melanin
Exuding passions
again and
again
How could I not get excited about that baby
How could I not

Imagine

You run through thoughts
Bare chest at best
Dust
kicked up past kneecaps
Running through
To
From
Coming undone
and reaching for
Another
Hands out stretched
Fingertips grazing molecules
Shifting components
Proponents to this love
Head tilted
Contemplating
Face kissed by sun's rays
I taste you
Bitter and chalky
Coiled tresses turn to assailant
my lip is recipient and yours be victim
and hearts beat in rhythm
in love

Embolden

Sometimes ignition
Sultry toxic
Invisible accelerant
Sets my surroundings ablaze
While I stand iced down
And amazed

Wet

Read a story about a man
Standing in the rain
A last rain
Death was his shadow
Light, a fading memory
But the rain
Drops tracing the lines of his face
Running along his body like a lover's hand

Last stand
Last intimate moment with the earth
If it were your last
How would you feel about the rain?

Birth

Creativity moving on the inside like the current of white water rapids
What is on the horizon for me
My spirit is calling pen and paper
My heart plays the soundtrack
To their relentless love making
Ideas coming out like the octuplet mom
But doubt has the birth canal blocked
So I'm welling up like toxemia
What is my release
What will give relief
What does my soul believe
That my heart is fearing
Not properly hearing
I need to connect
Got Mike Tyson swings
But life ducking me like I'm showing teeth

Appreciation

The road is long
Foreign objects penetrate our foundation
Making what was once stout
Void of steadiness
Visibility is low
The atmosphere plays favorites to obstruction

Come on Brotha

Young men stop surrendering your power
Relinquishing your crown
For the sake of being down
Don't be down, be up
Giving up your head
Translates to giving up your butt
Feeling like Bruce Willis
I wanna ask head or gut!
Brothas when are you going to think
Use your instinct
Before you are extinct
Your success is a bane
To the overseers existence
But when they tempt you to fall off
Be intelligent enough to resist it

And to all those Queens
Representing the family throne
Work your backbone
And keep your Kings on track
Before three steps forward
Becomes ten steps back
Wearing your past like dope head tracks
But the melanin can erase that
If you remember to be proud that you are black
Pride will remind you to persevere
Take forward motion while remaining reserved
Head up, and chest out
Because this fight of life has you enlisted
Don't resist it
Warriors are stubbornly persistent
But do not persistently pursue ignorance
Be clear

This world don't care
But I do
And your legacy's survival is dependent on you

Listen

What makes a human being starve their perfection?
Perceive criticism as rejection
Start with a collection
of things that are of
no benefit to the soul
stylish this and Donna Karyn that
NY lingo in your rap
But you reside in the suburbs of Connecticut
Fronting for who
related to what
Truth is light
and can be seen by the righteous
Black is your aura
Lacking is your ability to process thought
Learn what is taught
How can one understand without listening
What is the point of having ears
Half a vision is none at all
So when I call on you
to decapitate the perils of society
I don't want your Jolson impression
A simple expression
of the truth will suffice

My soul has not paid the price Black woman
Our people don't march no more

I know my nigga because my soul pays for you
and marching is too much of a chore
I'm just trying to give you guidance on what you should do
and what has worked in the past
may not be a necessity of the present
because presently the situations that are past

have past
and the new shit need a new fix
so don't tell me about yesterday
shut up and listen to what I'm trying to say
constructive analysis of modern day societal paralysis
is a tongue twister
look mister
I'm not talking for my health
I'm trying to do for self
but doing for me and my six
is inclusive of correcting you
and the ill shit you do
so I'm cautious to ask
what is the master plan
and what will you stand for or against
Political power is at our fingertips
but you can't see that
I'm trying to get you to hear me black
but your drum is suffering from a heart attack
and the Africa in your soul
whose responsibility it is to interpret and reconstruct the code
Has gone neglected and undetected
and my children will be affected
Now, when there's chance of you messin with mine
I got to step in
and reassemble your mind
wake up that which you keep sleeping
bring wisdom to your dome
like a jealous nigga creepin
old ladies peepin
and perspiration seepin
you might as well call it operation shake up
cause I won't shut up
fuck clothes
you got a house

is your name on a utility bill
don't even let keep it real fall from your lips
cause I'll drop you from your hips
I am sick and tired of ignorance
the shit is spreading like a California wildfire
90% of your body is water
but solutions ain't nothing
if you don't know the problem
you wit me
you hear me
ain't no need to fear me
For I am Truth
Listen

Beat Down

It's sad when I hear mothers perpetuating the stereotype
the stereotype that has a tendency to break our children
yelling at them because they want to laugh a lot
forcing them to sit down when they want to move
they want to groove
and your patience is thin
so you make their patience wane
because you have complaints
your child's struggle is NOT your struggle
believe it or not they have their own
I don't know about you
but I don't beat teenagers
you grown
that's a damn fight
so no, I am not in the business of
making my first reaction anger towards my seed
that's right!
I am not here to fight my child!
I am here to guide their wild
help them find their voice in the world
you wanna know where The Panthers and revolutionary fighters are?
Popping Adderall
getting yelled at and demeaned
or being beat by their parent in the street
We NEED every piece of the active and imaginative child
we need their fighting spirit
but if we as parents are allowing our fear of resistance
to stunt our children's social development
shame on you!
So since you scared they should be too!?
That is the sweetest shit I've ever smelt
accept the hand we are dealt
no, I am not one for stomping out a young warrior's spirit

I stomp out war songs
and call to arms
I stomp out the enemy
My God is a God of battle!
David's parents did not run down to the war and say
NO DAVID! You can't be throwing rocks at people!!!
THAT young boy STOOD TALL with authority when all the adults allowed
an army to call them out their name and disrespect their God!
He fought with ROCKS and words!

Now all of a sudden we don't throw rocks at our enemies anymore.
we coddle the dysfunctional relationships in hopes that
someone ELSE will come along and do the fixing for us

Anger

Festering; bubbling beneath the surface
you do not deserve your anger
A king answers to no one
is not driven by rage
but instead grows wise from the experience
fueled by life itself
taking each lesson and converting it
into what you need it to be
in order to secure your legacy
I hear it
I sense it
and some part of me is aroused
by furrowed brows
cold stern looks
a quick lashing of the tongue
words like samurai swords
and I, your Geisha girl
wrapped and bound
Knelt and curtsey
awaiting your orders
and if borders need invading
enemies fading
Throat circumventing
I am not remiss in mentioning
I serve my King
though almost scary
but
my darkness is drawn to your darkness
together
we shed light on it all
we will not fall
stand tall
release your all.....to me

The Nurturer

It's not about respect
Its about love
you are looking for one thing
yet perpetuating the other
snide and crude remarks
names that are not on my birth certificate
hurled like trophies
seeds planted by your hand
come out the ground and hit you
and you ask me why I watered the earth so
This is my soil and this is my sun
but the seed and the waters
children of your mouth
leaking legacies south
so when you north
and wonder why the sky rumbles so
understand
this be your planted land
and flying vegetables
of your own fruit stand

I am first: true divine order

No you aren't, I am. I am Queen Mother over them
You are Queen with Princess duties over me
complicated as this fairy tale be
It is
And now you wish to zip through
convoluted forests in pursuit of ever after
when there is laughter and folly and misgivings along the way
snares and traps and lies and hats
and things that could ruin your day
you cannot subvert
divert
Nor convert my followers
they don't change bloodlines
though fine, your line be diluted
in this Kingdom old ways are uprooted
it is a new day
one where your shadows are lost
In the light of my son
and the breasts of my daughters feed nations
as I sit and watch the development of a world
nurtured by my body
I cannot give you the crown
you dear mother
must learn to bow down

We Need More

I don't want to go into a bookstore that has ten thousand volumes and one shelf of 1900 books dedicated to African Americans, 110 books for Latinos and almost always this shelf is shared. However there is no Native American shelf. Their five books are blended in with ours. Herein lies the problem.
We need more books
I know we have stories
Volumes and volumes of stories waiting to be told
But you must tell them before you get old and
The weariness of carrying these tales becomes too much
and details turn into such and such

Hold Up!

Respect my militancy
You need my fight
Whether you think I'm wrong or right
don't toot your nose up
in disbelief because you do not think
there is a revolution going on

The news ain't new

HEY!
Has anyone seen a reporter?
you know those people who want you to know the truth
those people who smell a scandal and deception
jump into the lie
and bust it wide open like a watermelon hitting concrete
Those journalists that politicians hate to see coming
because they always have a tendency to discover their lies
and put they ass on front street
those people that made you pick up the newspaper
and after reading their article you felt enlightened
and if someone got away with injustice
the article you read was a form of vindication
Where they at though?
I keep seeing media whores
pimping time out to corporate America
selling smiles and celebrity bullshit
Who cares about your fake boobs
thirteenth husband, 12 adoption
no ovary having, drug addicted
ménage trois
I WANT TO KNOW WHAT IS HAPPENING
and the current climate of those appointed to provide the news
is feeding me defecation
while pissing on this nation
the television is a toilet
and the poets are here to flush it
spray authenticity in the air and open windows
we all have been smelling this steamy hot manure
so long some of us carry the smell on us
don't think your silence suppresses the smells
you may not speak but we smell the bull anyway
we must not allow these networks to continue contaminating the

airwaves
with their suggestive material
subliminally and overtly defining who we are as a people
you don't know me
and you should not prescribe to tell my story until you do
but if you don't have the time to seek the truth because
the networks have tightened your strings
and shined your tap shoes
then dance to the blues
because oppressed people across the world are rising up
and telling the story themselves
we don't need jaded reporters and sell-out journalists on our team
we have our own platforms
our own cameras
coming to you live this is T'Challa
the revolution is now
stay tuned

Brothers

others see you and only see your challenge
I see the beauty of your eye color
the joy of your laughter
your love for your big brother
and in turn his protection and care for you
As I sit in the concert hall
and listen to the joys of sound
coming from his mouth
and violas, violins and cellos
I cannot help but notice
how others tend to stare
as if this child should not be so
as if you are annoyed by his existence
why, he is a boy excited and eager about life
moved by the ebbing of horse hairs and wire
music like fire in his spirit causing bursts of excitement
the music stirs like a whirlpool
transporting young minds to the shores of other worlds
where their imagination can unfurl
but his short intermediate burst makes your toes curl
Why are we so eager to silence children?
Why do we want to schedule when they can express their joy?
happiness is not seasonal
or some occasional happening
so when someone, especially a child embarks on the edge of happiness
do not pull them back
set
them
free

Dark side

What's good?
Focused, no smiles
No random, meaningless conversation
Late night runs
Streets knowing the soles of your feet
And holding you up
Regardless of where you been
No concern for where you're going
Standing alone in support of your own
Just standing
In darkness
Position familiar
Though not a representative of current state
I relate
Not through experience
But I support my King
In darkness and in light
I don't pick and choose fights
I'm down for your cause
No matter where it leads you
Interceding prayers
Where I need to
Letting you know I am there
Here
For you
Loving you through
Awaiting the day
When you decide
To put Jeezy aside
For Miles
Meanwhile...I smile
And whisper
I love you...

Daylight

The sun lovingly shines
On you
Not because you are good
Or bad
Or even deserving
The sun shines because it wants to see you grow
If only
We could be more like the sun

MaMa

Why are you irritated by your child?
He is yours
at three he is exactly what you have groomed him to be
loud
screaming
stomping
disobedient risk taker
surely as you say don't leave the step
he and his confidant
bust the stairs and make it to the parking lot
with no pursuit or reprimand
so the child understands that your word is not bond
But you don't want to be bothered
because you don't have the patience or forethought to control your child
Yet, you get mad when the teacher calls
kind of like taking all your child's clothes off
so they can have dinner on a towel on the floor
ummmm
he needs to learn how to sit at the table,
patiently, and finish his meal
you are getting him accustom to a scenario that isn't real
people don't get naked to eat in a restaurant
so what is this gesture grooming him for?

What future are you preparing these young boys for?
What visions are you having for them?
did you dream while you incubated this child's brain
feed yourself books so he could gain
or were you too busy
for external nurturing
mama gotta have a life too
as this new life comes through the birth canal
your life goes to the back burner

you make choices for the benefit of your child
not your feminine wiles
or masculine desires
your objective should be higher
broader and more grand in scope
than anyone could hope
You are shaping a legacy!
Can't you see that?
You have the potential to set the mood of an entire generation
with your child
stop neglecting the intricate details of their future
have a vision
or prepare to take us all to hell

On Marriage

I don't have to be on the street to deal with
unwanted advances
no one talks about a wife's chances
sleeping peacefully
but awakened by phallus
accosted while eyes remain closed
I was not blind
and yet I find that I did not see this coming
rescued by the one thing I use to hate
swore she couldn't relate
always felt her timing was off
interrupted life leaving me scoff
but now I see
when I bleed
I am freed

A Silent Cry

moved to silent tears
as lyrics expressed fears
heartache floating on half and full notes
hope floats
but pain sinks
and to think
this tiny piece of life
heard the strife
and dropped tears down juicy cheeks
the heart speaks
and his heart listened
melodies told his heart a story
that unknown language expressed
and he responded physically
with water soaked cheeks
music explained something to him
and he understood
if only adults could be so fortunate
to journey through music like this tiny child

Moonlight

Rock of my love
energy source of everything that stirs me
moving emotion
like waves upon ocean
words watching over my soul
like moonbeams
their meaning, lingering
dropping seeds
Nourished by your movement
growing into blossoming trees
that sing your praise in sunlight
celebrating in every breeze
and honoring you in darkness
silently bowed in adoration
as your warming glow reassures
Your presence

Papers

My son got his papers
I was ecstatic at the fact
he can leave this country
then I realized
I don't have no papers
I don't have my papers
we all don't have papers
so we can't leave
how interesting
a country I do not rightfully belong to
has to give me permission to leave
they did not request permission for my entry
or that of my ancestors
they just took
and kept
and we wept
now we are left
to request permission

On dying

is it a form of giving up
or acceptance
releasing of aged flesh
a falling away
from the confinement of bone structure
accepting you have traveled this road
long enough
it is time to
is it time
time it is and time you must
learn and move
but do not rust

Sensory Overload

We see the world with
various parts of ourselves
all attentive to the moment
visualizing the dream
painting pathways to our goals
to the point where they are tangible
dancing with our fingers like water
sweet aroma of victorious love
filling our goblet as we toast to
futures mapped, pain capped

Punch Drunk

What is undone
Begun, and catapulted into your stratosphere
Wanting you close yet feeling you near
Longing for the words you speak
to rest upon my ear
So my spirit can dance in your atmosphere
Full of fear, but Danger girl
You make my heart unfurl
You take me to innocence
Remembering what was
Meditating on what could have been

My sin; Your sin
My chin; your shin
Blend and bend and taste again
waters that nurture so
love that makes inspiration grow
Trapped in a vegetable garden
With the beauty of a rose
Leaning your way as if searching for sunlight
Really just wanting to be loved right
Can one outgrow what was thought to be forever
Once you realize you & another should be together
Though paths took us to two different states
State of mind we cannot fake
Desire now channels our fate
A love denied will be had
Spirit unclad, heart cloaked in you
Love dripping from my chest like morning dew

I Sing

I sing & colors paint the sky
Glimmer hits my eye
I sigh & inhale
Swallowing deep breaths of you
Hum melodies and tones
Paint hues to subdue
Sing love to the bone
Minor flaws condoned
Stroke air as if close
Lean and feel surges to my toes
Trapped in the fiber of my being
Released in the power of my singing
A love released for the world to hear
The realness of passion that is you my dear
Unforgettable
Undoubtable
memorable
Such a delectable stain

Summer

Red Clay

You no longer maintain the rich buoyancy of your past
Evergreen roots within you do not last
Crimson tone expressing your history
Some locations contents remain a mystery

But I see

Where hearts cry out
Youth Sacrificed
Wombs Commandeered
Women nurturing their oppressor
Never made the lesser
 It is my blood that flows through your veins
Loosening chains

If you listen

You can hear the jilted lover
Angered at passions unreciprocated
Though legs be liberated
Hearts do not surrender
Scholars consistently evade the truth
While pictures contain selective memory
Emphasized by Willie notes
Laced with Disney style stories
And watching hope float

Literacy be hot
Even when truth is not
But I seek you
No matter how frigid
You playing invalid
To this Queen's resurrection power

Rise up
From this wretched Georgia clay
Today is the day

Revelations

The Resilient

Coastal borders forged in search of greater opportunity
Leaving what was, in search of essential unity
Fighters, dreamers, thinkers, inventors
Motivated human beings seeking to do better
Seeking to be better
In search of
No weapon formed against them could deter them from their path
America, they thought
That is where our life will begin
The apple; said their hunger
They dug deep
Deep until they changed color and reflected the beauty of the A-train
They sweated until their visions stood tall
And you saw their empire state of mind
They were kind when need be
And aggressively passionate
Barriers circumvented
Unrelenting
Growth
Can't stop won't stop
You are the city that eats adversity
You are the people that build when they say it is impossible
You are the people that live when the rest of the world is dying
So what I ain't got it – that's just right now
But you wait
I'm calculating moves and initiating investments
Maneuvering through this cesspool of polygamist ideologies and focusing
on the extreme
Blessing my seed – till my hands bleed
With tenacious diligence, efficient strategies, masterful management,
tangible prosperity
That's my legacy
I'm a New Yorker – can't no storm see me!

Progeny

I bleed your love
reflected on gratitude
and realized I get full off you
so full in fact that
if sliced
or grazed
by slight of page
my blood would cry out your name
again and again
to the tune of a Sam Cooke song
it won't sing long
you would find your way
back into my veins so we could
flow together once again

Fair Trade

When life makes you scream
I will cause you to whisper
when life gives you gas
I will patiently await your slow digestion
when life makes you angry
I will be your calm

You gave me life with those
Six words
It's as if energy from my I love you
Returned re-surged
by your love
refueling me for the next couple of hours
until your voice does what your words do
sooth my desire
calm my passion
and curb my appetite
and at the very least
satisfy my inner beast

Clemency

I wanna be free!
But I can't get you to see past me
And
Into these facts swimming in an ocean of lies
Is justice still justice when the wrong person dies
Is justice still justice when an action is taken
Life mistaken and lives shaken
Is justice still justice when you have to come back
And after you act say, "oops, my bad I thought you were someone else."
"We just had to move, people wanted results."

death plus death leaves nothing left

Emptiness and quiet rooms
Wanting to spend time where memory consumes
Heartache looms and solid theories are questioned
Leaving you second guessing
With seconds less

Tick

Tock

Heart

Stops

But my belief makes it beat
Passion puts me on my feet
I take a stand
A stand for what I believe; reprieve
I believe in justice
I believe in the pursuit of truth

There was once intimacy between the two and though no super sleuth
It is clear; justice hasn't always liked me
Or my brotha
Or brethren of color
She is a lover of self
Prideful and egotistical
Sarcastic and cynical
She doesn't always believe that I am innocent
until proven guilty
before a court of law
She doesn't always see to it that I am tried before a jury of my peers
For she is blind and she fears me
Fears my strength and ability
But no matter how much she denies me
I am her saving grace
A constant reminder of who she once was
And the precursor to her fate

Shout out to the mothers

The mothers who are whispered to
in brightly lit places
colorful faces
man made
to the mothers who got played
to the mothers who said no
to the mothers who said no but stayed anyway
to the mothers who have no more words to say
got to your – this –is-my-last-day stance
finished with your dodge-the-swings dance
to the mothers that didn't finish
dreams not quite diminished – just rocking on that back burner
to the mothers that revolt like Nat Turner
to the mothers sitting in jail cells
to the mother that almost was
and to the mother of many
to the mothers that can't get enough of that
good and plenty
to the tricking mothers
to the ticking mothers
to the who the hell you looking at like that – I know you got skeletons in
your closet too bitch – step off for you get your ass beat out here in these
streets- kind of mothers
to the peaceful turn the other cheek mothers
to my mothers in love with other mothers
to the mothers that started off as otha lovers
to the flawed, imperfect, everybody room clean but yours- kind of
mothers
to the come here and hug me forget them chores kinda mothers
home be an open door kind of mothers
love on all the children in the hood
cause her womb be her heart
and she birth the art of love

To all you women
that nurture life
be it birthed physically or spiritually
I thank you
thank you for sharing your very nature
with the world

The moral of the ... Really?

What story is this?
Who came up with this insidious plot?
Are you joking?
Disgust provoking
Failures choking
Is my soul smoking?
What is really going on?
Where is the theme song?
Is this movie three hours long or a mini-series?
Are we evaluating the human condition?
Or pontificating theories
I mean really
Is the writer dyslexic?
The middle ends with the beginning
The plot is thinning
And the antagonist is heroically fighting
Against my pro's con
You trying to subdue my reason
Subjugate my feasibility into more you and less me?
Why?
You don't like me?
Does anyone even care?
Do you dare test me that way?
What can you say that will deduce me to less than a Queen?
I mean
Whose story is this anyway?
I mean really!
Are ya trying to piss people off?
Leave them scoff
Gibing at the actions of a Saint
Envious of what you ain't
Trying what you can't
End these meanderings

You are writing
Writhing
Squirming through your main event with discontent
Your plot I circumvent
I am the Pi of ciphers
A cryptographer's muse; and you lose

Bae

You trying to make me like you or something?
Man. I ain't got time to like you!
Shit...It's hard enough liking myself
and here you come grinning and carrying on like
What up Bae?
What's up witchu?
No really, what is, up with you?
You liking me,
but are you doing you?
Or is pursuit alone supposed to make me swoon
Food ain't free and neither is time
But I continue to find
Both these things in route to you
I am not easily cajoled
And though I had no intentions of even knowing you
My heart is true
Don't dance with me
if you got no shoes

Closed for Cleansing

But not as closed as I should be
Pumper still open
Humper still coping
Drawn into others
As self stretches beyond its borders
I can't hear her though
My fake ass laugh too loud
Body knows what's necessary
Stop and flow
tensions released
Emotional spasms
Replace orgasms
Silence is meditation
but so is talking

Stout

Embracing every meal that takes hold of me
Embracing the beauty of age
While hairs center stage
Took forty years to embrace my femininity
With maturity
Accepting me
My desires and likes and healthy appetites
Whatchu know about this brown eyed vixen
Fixin to lay this
Libra love on you
Searching to unleash this royalty
On my King
A legacy bequeathed
Empires birthed by your girth
Nurtured by the wisdom of the ancients

Slow Down

Don't be asking me for pictures
and poses
and various exposures of my physical display
don't approach me that way
requesting tango sessions
what that mouf do lessons
and guesses at my level of freakdom
don't flash me your phallus
and ask me my fantasies
so you can take parts of me home with you
where you live out voyeuristic dreams
and porn fantasies
you so caught up in visual stimulation
you have yet to ponder
connecting to my mental
and that oversight is consequential
wanting access without completing the prerequisite
you have to earn entrance to other levels
and your ass still at the front door
wondering what you even came around for
cause I seem to be playing games
nigga I'm Milton Bradley
you just a hat on the board
I ain't trying to sew no discord
but I need you to be informed
mama generous and stingy
how the scale tips
has nothing to do with me
Choose wisely

Say No More

Walked to my car door just full of smiles
subdued immediately by feminine wiles
I smiled
amused by your charm
and seeing no harm
I rolled and rolled
and you told and told
snippets of your story
didn't bore me
just kept a smile on my face
I kept pace
and kept feeding your greedy ass
greeting you with sass
and...Popeyes
can't tell you why
time flies
but it seemed as if no time passed at all
I stall
you call
aroused slightly by full lips
and lip licks
and laughter; we chatter and stare
and I don't care
I have no intentions of loving you
but you don't give a damn
you just wanna know
but I ain't saying
you think I'm playing
but when invitation leads you to my door
your reply
Say. No. More.

This Love

This love
This love
I cannot shake, break, or fake
I cannot turn away from
I cannot replace with other tastes
Assimilate or commingle
There are no carbon copies or duplications
It is
Always will be
the love that was meant for me.
If it wasn't meant to be
I wouldn't have found you when you were looking
Seeking each other out
Our love moves us when we are not conscious
Gravitating thoughts to the place where we both exist
In passionate bliss
Our time spent is a young girl's dream
One from which I do not wish to wake
I grow when we partake
Heart aches when
Reality is fake
Diminishes my dreams in its shadows
Some may see my actions shallow
Be that as it may
My heart shall not release you
This day or any other to come
Fruitful and dreaming of bearing
And rearing
But that is the second part of my dream

I'm Smitten

Passion gets me every time
I can't complain
But as desires build my repertoire
I find I want you more
Denied access for so long
Refused to believe, for you
I longed
Yet here I am
After one taste
Unable to lose your face
Eyes captivated by beauty's gaze
Caught up in this maze
Seeking to be chased
The act was no disgrace
Just
Correct placement
Now our souls connected
No longer neglected
Eternally reflected
I didn't get away
Just came back another day

Nothing

When I sit and contemplate
you pose question on activity
wanting simply to speak with me
something many suitors forget to ask
simple in task
seconds in labor
and you savor the work
each day checking to see what I would say
then one night
I answered
Nothing
and you posed I do nothing
with you
sit
with you
breathe
with you
so we sat
and did nothing together
did not even speak about the weather
you coped a quick touch
nothing too much
enough to make me laugh
as always
and that day
we connected
as I reflected
on nothing

Link up

Imma need you to focus a lil better
On how you connect and fetter
Yourself to me
The hands hold till they sweat or cramp
Legs connect in certain atmospheres
But what we have here
Is a tie to our souls
But your soles acting old
Like walking is not what they were made for
Motions be on reserve
Emotions I can't conserve
So my heart dangles
Anger in tangles with passion
Now you have a woman on a rampage
Passion fueled by rage
Flipmode be the greatest
But flipping should be the last thing
You want me to do
Flipping my heart to another
From you
Flipping my bottom
To the top for a new boo
All because you failed to properly connect
Filled my heart with neglect
Now my mind elects the attentive and erect
While you deflect
Yet expect vulnerability
All that good shit you felt when you first met me
And my heart is closed
In the end you want to talk
But when I needed it your mouth was shut
Now my soul is sealed—up like the windows of heaven
To fallen angel

Cut me and your own heart dangles
Torn flesh and gaping wounds
Healed by a touch from you
But are you reaching
Speaking
Leaking your hearts desires into my eardrum
Close enough for me to hear your heart hum
Before it is too late
I need you to contemplate
Think before I reach my brink
And permanently sever this link

Say what now?

This damn world is too small
Was up a lil bit and had to fall
back
Played around
And found
distance is not far
And in the oddest of places
You find what you lack
Comfortable like we go way back
Clowning like you know me like that
Cool as cousins
Wished we wasn't
Ignorance can be a nut
If you let it
Hard to forget it
Cain't regret it, shit
Ya lil strong ass
Held tight, upright
Returned my fight
And even spit on it right
In light
Of this new information
Of this possible relation
I cry foul, I mean...
Fuck it, we all family now

R & R

Seemly and befitting
I am
Though a little bougie at times
Never too good for the hood
But my uppity moments be consistent
So I just don't resist it
Don't let the political correctness mislead you
Though professional in any arena
I will drag your hoe ass on some straight R and R
What?!
You just gone sit there and act like
You don't wanna whack dumb people across they brow
Cause they gave you a headache
When you were trying to figure out
HOW
How can a muthafucka be this dumb
Is your brain numb
Come here and let me kick you in your ass
See if that makes you move fast
I know when I need R and R
Niggas be fine
Well not really but that imprint
So distinct
I can't help but think
You probably look real good
With your face underneath me
What!?
Can't we all get head?
Ahead
Some head
You know what the fuck I mean!
And R and R ain't what you think
Its what I like to call

A return to the nature of a thing
No filtering
It gives me so much peace
When I have ratchet release
Gotta let that bitch breath from time to time
Cause if she come out without no parameters in place
Somebody feelings gone be displaced
And a smug bitch might get slapped in the face
Therefore to maintain balance in my atmosphere
I let that hoe go free three times a year
Just hope she don't get us locked up again
Or unauthorized access to multiple parties
Or showing the freaky to men who can't handle
Just one sample
They the worst cause you can't shake them niggas!
Anyway
Don't be stingy okay
Let your ratchet, ghetto, unfiltered, unapologetic
Not from concentrate
Raw and organic material
Break forth
Be naturally you
Even if that be some ratchet ass shit boo-boo!

Until

There are people that we say we love
Yet
Reaching out to tell them
Is something we pass on
Not
Me
I need you to know how I feel
Know when you cross my mind
When your fragrance causes my head to
turn
Only to find, you're not there
I need you to know when I am sitting alone
Feeling some kind of way,
thoughts of you light my face
To the point where memory is re-lived as if
it were just this morning
Smiling through,
I forget why I felt funky
in the first place
Things like baths
Amusement parks
Gifts
Glances of a young girl's crush
Stares of a woman's lust
Gripping sheets from firm thrusts
Memories
Like these...never fade
They replay
serve purpose by brightening my day
setting passions to a blaze
So much so that
I bleed on blank pages
Until the onslaught of words

Cause poetic orgasms
And
I
am
satisfied
Until the next time

To Die For

One thought
One mention
Full on all levels
Passions elevated and set aflame
From one phrase
My arms
MY
Arms
Cradle you from this world to the next
You would have no worries relinquishing
In my presence
And you are right
I would sing your praises
And carry you in my bosom
The same way I hold you in my heart
Giving you my very breath
until
I have
nothing left
As the idea of not having you
makes me weak

Drifting

My mind falls on you often
I think about the first time I opened myself up to you
I wanted you to be the first to ever see me
I experimented, and, they tickled a bit
But never hit it, and you were Hank Aaron
Evidenced by cherry juiced sheets
Mission complete
Predecessors never came to my incision
But you made provisions for my decision
You talked with me bluntly
And made sure I was sure
No pressure to endure
You knew what you wanted
And knew I wanted you
And some days I still do
But our time has come and past
And come and passed
And come and passed and if our paths cross again
Only time will tell
Compelled by thoughts of your shoulders
Silk playing in the background
And us playing in the foreground
Soft murmurs and songs sung
I was sprung
A love that started with you will not end
I still consider you my friend
Someone I was completely honest with...
Open with
Sadly enough you were not ready
To truly embrace the love I had to give
If so, you would have been able to step out and come to me
As I came to you
I can still see you in your brown leather jacket

At your locker by the stairs
Looking at me, smiling
Not knowing how open my heart would be to you
How true
The last time you said it was like a fantasy
It was ecstasy to our own soundtrack
I think back to college girl
Surprising visits
And yet the most memorable
Is the night you rode your bike to my house
Just because you wanted to see me
The act means so much
I can feel the heat from your touch
See you singing on stage at the concert
Embrace our love for music and how much it impacted
Those memorable moments we shared
I still care
Always will
I am your Juliet
And you are my…….

Answering Machine

Automated nobody
Dodging unwanted conversations
Fostering dissention in relations
Misinterpreted correlation
Leading to partner cancellation
No refunds
Personal invisible liar
Saving me from solicitation
And calls from folks who can't
Get no higher
Blind to our unification

Just Say No

Subliminally volunteered
Internally, I sneered
Didn't no, 'Yes' fall gracefully from my lips
These hips lied
Mouth sighed
And pupils dipped to corners
Don't adorn you
Disdain at your request
But you approach as pleasant and pleasing
So sugary sweet
I get caught seizing

Blissful Kisses

Blissful kisses
of former Mrs.
causes the heart to reminisce
patiently longing
for other's belongings wrongly
but far from a thief
more like a repo man
taking what I can
When emotional default is seen
No need to enforce liens
Seeing that standards have not been met
causes other goals to be set
never living for regrets
I'm going for what I can get
Working to reach higher achievement
But desired bereavement is
Somewhat unattainable
plots thicken but still unnameable
hearts quicken but still unclaimable
what I do to you old women would find shameable
I aim for it though
got new tricks I wanna show
time made that little gold heart grow
you know who's it is
you know who this is
and we not kids
time for grown folk biz
without a pre-test or a quiz
You the first and only student
with the only syllabus
Knew Mrs. When she was still a Miss
Soul swishes when you are near to this
I persevere to fulfill your every wish

longing to satisfy your soul as you grow old
just please take head to this
the message is never a miss
on target like a marksman
cause you spark my inner bliss
kissing blissfully
entering me
I'm secure like Fort Knox
I enjoy making your soul rock
There's a section of your heart I have on lock
I ponder, often wonder
Does distance make the heart grow fonder
forced conversation when you really want relations
in many positions and kinky locations
front seat or rear we've been there
and sometimes I fear
your love will undoubtedly draw me near

Seated

It happened in the car
Didn't intend for it to happen that way
But
You were staring at me
That way you do
Hands held
Words expelled
Then
Your look changed
From admiration
To adoration
Adulation
You leaned in and the kiss
Almost did not touch me
Then slight pressure
Melted into a slow tongue dance
While our bodies were break dancing!
But we couldn't
Not
there
So you drove because
We were at that point
I needed you to know
To feel

This real
Beating for you
Secreting for you
Soft brown
Heated
Replete
True, for you
Tempered

Rhythmic
To soft melodies
That played out like
your favorite theatrical love scene
soft nibbles
long stares in amazement
at the beauty
that is our love
caress
confess
nestled in the crease of my neck
held as close as possible
until the fire of me
melts the ice of you
and rest in my love
cradled by passion
suffocating in fealty
...
Is
that
the police?
   'What's going on here?'
Blushes
'We, we were just talking...'
   'I think I know what's going on. You
two get moving.'
Yeah...
good times!

Ebony Sunrise

You are my knight in shining armor
We do not subscribe to European tales
We are African
So when you rescued my trodden heart
Made love art
And spoke my native tongue
Till all the damage was undone
Your love removed the veil of deception
And to my recollection
Elevated my status
Dusted off my crown
Bowed down and lifted me up
The view from here made it clear
I do not make you a King
You were born royalty
Your mother gave you the key
And with it
You unlocked me

Oh

So you thought you had me pegged
since you touched my head
and discovered my coif be softer than yours
stronger than yours
kinda how my melanin shines brighter
born fighter
got Africa in my roots
and a butterfly in my boot
Don't come for the Queen!

I'm not one for comparing
but got DAMN you always staring
Got disdain all in ya tone
wish your fake ass would leave me alone
But you can't help but be drawn in
by what you wish to achieve
throwing all this salt
when it is ME you wanna be
I know
My game is tight
mind right
money long
and Kingdom building skills be decades strong
I could play your ass like a Keith Sweat song
you pry and you spy but you ain't slick
deep down inside, I know you ain't shit

You know it too
So imma sit perched on my throne
letchu do what you do
But when these earrings come off
I'd hate to be you

Alignment

Stars align
so they work cohesively and in synch
I think
When contemplating universal things
and seeing beings
as sources of energy
my chi
is inappropriately aligned
there are curves
where right angles should be
No longer can yours be with mine
I be sunshine
you be black hole
syphoning from soul
lack of resource impairs vision
and can fuck up the whole mission
cause toxic conditions
and murderous intentions toward dreams and renditions of things to
come

You are bright colors
beautiful sounds
the happy side of nature
you are the trickle of fresh water springs
down quiet creeks that have yet
to be discovered
content in solitude
you are the strength of the Baobab
Fire resistant
persistent in the face of adversity
you helped give birth to the truest essence of me
you are
by far

the most significant man I have ever loved
I met a King once
His name was hebrew
I was forever marked by his love

Lost and sought out
contact so damned subtle it whispered
my spirit heard you
and humming bird wings
clapped your name
wind blew love
that sparked flames
now fire consumes
passion be fueled repeatedly
yet we are gods
Eating anar
and allowing our love to burn
indefinitely
the way it did when it lit our paths
to each other

Untitled

Inhale deep; breathe
try not to picture chocolate skin
chiseled face bears no expression
just the suggestion
of being pursued
hard working hands that applaud
the softness of me
confidence dominating my space
beard brushes my face
aggression subdued by lotions
gentle moan like potions
calling to the wild
essence riled
lust inducing intoxication
staunch sweat from lewd positions
I open to you
remove your blindfold
and shove you into the depths of my caverns
sit if you dare
make yourself comfortable

Fingertips

Fingertips in my mouth
life falling from my chin
happy to end
only to begin again
lust boiling beneath my surface
atop waves of emotion, you ride
desires I no longer hide
hungry for the moisture of you
bent over and receptive
uninhibited
break skin,
shiiiiiiit!
I do it all for the taste of you
fingers in my mouth
hand upon my waist
pillow in my face
shhhhhhhhhhh
Go 'head; take it girl
take it all
gladly, I accept
and lick and swallow
gulp and chug
slurp and suck
You
through
Every entry of me
then I'll rest you on my bosom
where you regain energies
nurtured god

Harmony

I am your cello
Your fingers strum my melody
Make me hum highs and lows
Vibrations make secretion; inevitable
Cumming to your music
Infused with our love
Riding a never ending beat

Wedding Band

She still wears the ring
Remnant of a love that spanned decades
One that still shines warm light
In the darkness of solitude

Observe

I notice nature when I think of you
Witness life
See it as it happens
Reflected on
as I am so much alive
Memories of you stir my heart like
Spoons to warm chilli
Desiring to stick to your bones
And fill you

Love

Black love is a resilient thing
It sticks through the hardest of times
Shows the beauty in rhyme
Shines light on
What others ignore
Gives no hint to what's in store
But swells with anticipation
One smile brings elation
Each day is a cause of celebration
I know
Because
I'm serving black love daily
Come getcho' plate baby

On

I wanna taste your mouth
Get close enough
To press my body against yours
Trying to cop a feel
Laugh because
My moves are lame
And I can't contain
This bold love
This boisterous playmate
She is high off your sweetness
Humbled by your meekness
Amazed your eyes
Still hold childlike wonder
Unable to resist this spell I'm under
Underestimated
And overwhelmed
The rumble of your vibration
Compels
The sway of my legs
Then rolls around my head
And begins aligning my chakras

I didn't know how off balance I was
Had no idea
Your energy would be key
To me
Did not fathom my atoms transference
Be inference to my soul
Awakening what once was old
Bringing my truest self to light
Showing the beauty of this love is right

Flix

Four letters
Coveting our deepest form of erotica
I watch
I stop
Dirty thoughts walk nude
In patent leather shoes
Four inches above morality
Testing my mortality
Folks cutting to the chase
Putting ass to face
I take popcorn to debauchery
Sometimes that is the mood for me
Perverse curse and spit
Shit
Don't act like you look away
As if prude did not intrude
On your freedom
Don't be ashamed of your
Desire to view copulation
Education is essential
And knowledge fundamental
To your advancement in this field
Why should you yield?
It's how we all arrived
We need mere masters in the field
Too many novices
Perpetrating the fraud
Jesters; talking like they sex gods
Whatchu thought
One peak would leak eons of climactic wisdom
Into your mental prism
Push out misgivings and misconceptions
Replace limp with

Pharaoh like erections, envision
Temples of homage to your greatness

I hate to be late and break this fantasy
But you sitting on the couch just like me
Smirking at every titillating tit
Aroused by every moisture inducing flick

The Color of My Flowers

I do no pick them
That's selfish
But I love their colorful spread
Turning heads
Showing comfort to those
Bedridden
stricken
facing vacant side of bed
One does not unpluck another
Cut root of brother
But blossom and shine
Benign

Intimacy

Intimacy
Newly defined and refined
Nothing sexual about it
But an evolution
No doubt
It is heart spilled out
in correspondence
history told
cards unfold
pictures and artwork
and books and movies
and
music; the perfect backdrop
old, sultry, ballads
crooners making hearts swoon
and knees buckle at the
emotional exposure
I keep my composure
And sit at bar counter
Gaze into tired eyes
That still hold surprise
Smile from joy filled soul
Kiss hand
And understand
It is all love

Fall

Seasonal

Cold and barren
clearing out the dead and killing the weak
while whitewashing the process
saturated by what we need
restricted by what we see
and then
colors burst forth
and all about
reminding us of sacrifice
sunrise servants
giving salutations and hallelujahs
nothing compares to the freedom cry of children
running from structure to liberty
night kept at bay
while children and adults play with light of day
and warmth of night
yet life requires a return of sorts
we don down feathers and leathers
layers to protect sun kissed skin
as earth shows her varying hues
the push of wind thrusting through and clearing out the departed
once again
barren forests exposed
nighttime grows
what once welcomed all
is now frigid and closed
selective
all subject to pruning
become reflective
when life becomes suggestive
while time forces you to move
somber solitude
housing hearts and minds and contemplations

translates to resistance

though capable of giving you strength and revelation

it makes me a widow to love

cloaks me in darkness

isolation so loud it gives me a headache

stomach churning from the loneliness

shoulders aching from the tension

of holding myself up, when I wanna fall down

strewn before you

With my motives in hands

cupped together and surrendering

the softer side of me

hopeful

plodding

praying

that your vision be clear and certain

desires aimed at someplace close to me

and not just in my vicinity

respite shows me something...

else

decades have passed

alas comes understanding

two years

eight seasons and expectancy feels like complacency

if closed lips spoke

would value be birthed

knowledge of what you've unearthed

advising you

of that which you possess

I am a mess

wanting you

Morning

Orange seeping through blue hues
Evidence of brighter tomorrows
So sealed in the moment
That I do not recall breathing
One seagull flapping its wings
Celebrating its freedom
Or applauding passions shared
We stared
I felt your heart beat against my back
Felt myself back on track
And yet
Longing not to be separate
From my heartbeat
your heartbeat
in synch at sunrise

Beat

Thump thump
My ear magnified the beat
Sheets encased heat
Lulled by the rhythm of you
Faint silhouette
Silver wisdom dancing from chest to chin to crown
Hypnotized by your breath
Burrowed in your depth
Safe and secure
Exclusively your demure

Why we eat so much bullshit?

I mean
I like chips and chocolate
But in the wake of the New Year
All you, wanna live healthier folks
Got me second guessing what I enjoy the most
But then again
I can't feel guilty about my love affair with Utz
Shoot
We close like that
The green bag gets me
When people forget me
Neglect me
Fail to reflect on the importance of me
I subtract myself from their feed
And feed my mouth
A chip
No chip on my shoulder
Just in my hand
But only for a second
Make feelings disappear
Just like this chip
Fades behind full lips
See
We have an understanding
So you get with your meal planning
Set yourself up for the weeks ahead
Ill place these thoughts together
And weather this phase
With a bag of Lays
Utz understands
I'm not a brand whore
Just like the contents of that mostly air filled bag
So

Let me go
My chips calling me

righteous

Eyes decline
Broad grimace
Fingers entwine
Shrewd edifice
Rapid palpitation
Hand closing in
Dryness of mouth
Proximity of sin

Up the road

So close
But can't inhale your exhale
So close
elbows do not bump
So close
yet unable to make out your pores
nose does not brush nose
toes caress no calf
hands do not know half
eyes that wander room
love that looms

Untitled

Two years of periodic encounters
the inevitable found us
made what was two into one
creation
Elation
How my soul celebrated your presence
My body rejoiced and reacted to the sound of your voice
Then a choice
That has me empty and missing you all the more
Hoping you come strong again and knock upon my door

the start of it all

I can remember the first taste
The flavor
The shape and feel on my tongue
Pink and dense navigation
Arresting my nose
Never once thought molestation
Just following orders
Exploited curiosity
Aroused at the chance to explore
But not really knowing what I was used for
I remember opening it up
And taking direction
Now mature and in recollection
Of this natural pull that takes place
Small fire or roaring blaze
Sincerely desired or passing phase
Virgin mother or sex slave

Prisoner of war

Taken
But not in that sense
Past tense but present
As an adult
And adolescent
Had me at
Full eyebrows
Curly hair
You look away
I stare
I pull back
And you bare
Look at us
No fuss
No cuss
Just pure laughter
Unrelenting awe
Hand upon jaw
Heart thawed
Melted love
seeping through pores
Open doors
Closed windows
You chose
I rose

Mountains

Cold tips
Peaked and snow capped
Standing in confidence
Above valleys of dismay
Sunrise and set as backdrop
Silent while visions speak profoundly
Strength abounding

History

I love my ancestors
By definition
Silver haired
Hunched over carriers of the past
Eyes telling stores the mouth has ceased to speak

Hands bearing the marks
Of holding someone else's load and yours too

Untitled

If I was there
close to you
I'd bring you that steak
and this ass
and anything else you desired to get you through your day
nothing would stand in my way
no obstacle or element or human being
would prevent me from loving you through action
I am determined to give you all of me

Little one

I see you everywhere
tucked in watered eyes
rolling around small mouths
trapped in laughter
I see arms reaching for me
lips on my cheek
embraces that don't quite make it around my neck
arms too short
legs too little
you must be carried
but my back gave out
and I gave up before I even started
now I walk around broken hearted
seeing you everywhere
locked in your stare
wondering what questions you ask
when eyes lost in thought
hypnotize my heart

On My Terms

The creative
We thrive off change
Consistency is the devil
When it clashes with the freedom of creativity
We are persistent in our craft
But the norms of the world are the enemy
We live to stir the pot
Force a new way of thinking
Because everything their teaching
Is not reaching anyone at all
Organizational structure
Has imagination on haldol

You Don't Own Me

I remember my mother telling me
How wonderfully
And beautifully made, I be
Woven together with histories
Kissed with ancient mysteries

I remember her gazing into my eyes
The joy on my father's face as I laughed
His precious, I am
I remember

I remember the warmth of their presence
Heads turning when I entered the room with them
The world knew who I belonged to
I donned their love for me
Wore it like a royal cloak

Then in you came
Attempting to choke and stifle
Battle my memories like long lost rivals
Replacing my joys with your deceptive gain
Come on man
You not loving me
You not wanting what's best for me
Unfortunately you not able to see
Beyond your own pain
Subjecting me to the ramifications
Of your own rejection
But from my recollection
My DNA has no trace of you
No first birthday photo
Bike assembly
Barbie dream house parental nightmare

No Easter photos
Or holidays
Don't play
Your title not daddy
Then you wanna tell me
Don't wear this
Don't go there
Don't do that with your hair
Where you going
Who you with
I don't have time for this oppressive shhhhh

I have been awakened by an unconditional
That's become situational
dissecting subsection and constituent
evaluating current conditions
and causing decommission of the irrelevant

I been listening!
I heard him say
I was the apple of his eye
The reason he put the stars into the sky
Then he gave me the world
And even though I messed up
He continued to fill my cup

So when you bring your raggedy butt
Trying to redefine and realign me
While sipping from my cup
Invading my peace with your grief
And demeaning me
Embarrassing me in front of your friends to NO end
Then thinking after all that hurt
my yoni
Is your universe for you to mishandle and misuse

I will NOT be abused
That's not what my father built me for
I am a help but I will NOT help you destroy me
I am not your property
I am a child of the MOST high King
He sent me here as a Queen
with authority and dominion
So you can keep all your opinions
You will not disrespect
Neglect
Or expect to see me circumspect
You will love me like my God loves me
Unconditionally
Or you will let me be
But one thing is for sure

You
Don't
Own
me

Silence

Distant gaze into
Neverland
Decked out in bright colors
Though creeping into darkness
Cold moist places
Where brisk wind
Blows holes
And toes sense danger coming
Hearts echo bellies rumbling
Dusting off suit jacket
So thoughts be presentable
Walking them back and fourth
In my cerebellum
So concepts plentiful
But shame and guilt
Keep trying to abort my vision
So here I am sitting
In silence
Moving wind through circular energies
Trying desperately
To center me
Bringing my strength under submission
But doubt is fishing
Thoughts swimming trout style
While current carries me south

Manual constraint

Nose erect
some neglect
My tongue won't even get wet
And yet
Confounded
Compounded
And completely surrounded
In solitude

I conclude
The end be a means
Ill take these things
Leave that
Don brimmed hat
And knap sack
And attack pavement
Desert enslavement
Seize enfranchisement

Embrace myself
Been running too long
And she and I must
Talk
Can't embark on futures
Addressing old sutures
Fortifying man made boundaries
Bounce check on dowries
With self-imposed embargo
Holding heart as cargo
I know
but I don't stay
Gotta do what others don't
Be content in my own space

Walls surrounding
Audience to an exclusive screening
Resulting in me sitting
in my own fluids
Played myself into a puddle thinking of you
Hearts in synch
Focused
always coming back to that
one
Single
Thought

I love you

Resonating through radio waves
Dancing from audio to visual

I love you

Pronounced as if pledging allegiance
Besieged by your compassion
Subject to accepting rations knowing I want
To ravish just as much as you want to devour
Counting hours
Till I get back to my love

Speaking to the goddess

Niggas be trippin!
Want all the loving
While still pimping
In all actuality you a simpleton
Women be trying to give your ass a chance
And on second glance
You didn't deserve the opportunity to begin with
Unworthy opponent
Faulty components
Coming in like you had a winning season
When you really just a wildcard
With a participant trophy
You not even worthy to hold me
Gave a half-assed effort
And barely got yourself in the yard
Now that you happened to be staring at the goddess
You get braggadocios
Swole chest like pride be a bulletproof vest
Smiling as if your effort got you here
When your ass need to be trembling in fear
Always moving with selfish intentions
As if my anger won't leave you in stitches
Hungry and wanting and unloved,
you needy little bitches
I can tell by your talk what you trying to get
Though motives be exposed you still won't quit
Acting like your shit is legit
And undetected
Just because you sat in the garden for a spell
Don't make you its keeper
More like an earthworm
Tilling the ground
Till that real and true seed bearer

Comes around
And so what if I let you hit
between my legs ain't it
That's merely the beginning of the journey
But your trip gone be short lived
Took when you should have tried to give
Apologies and I love yous
Do not make my heart subdue
Lies be elevation
Changing my point of view
Showing me you
Exposing the darker sides you try to hide
But all things are exposed in time
In the face of your own truth
You grasp for my reality
Thinking I was present was a fallacy
Understanding coming to you so late
Gave me time to contemplate
Meditate on your inaction
How you ration
What you lack and
How this happened
You see severance in my eyes
Don't act surprised
Don't be trying to stake claim
Got your arrow tempting to aim
But my heart is on refrain
See, you still under observation
Though we had relations
The lesser me believes in your potential
But the greater has seen how loving potential
Is essentially love's quietus
Passion's riotus
oblivion
So I implore you

Don't approach me in vain
The injury to your soul,
won't allow your heart to regain consciousness
The goddess will leave you confined in your own mess
And the love you ignored
Be my egress

Theorizing Pontificates

I will not be limited to the confines of someone else's vision. Do not attempt to limit me to the construct of your reality. What is truth but a myth you have determined to believe as true. In that regard we manifest our own realities. In the most basic of terms, your life is what you make it out to be. It is within your hands and you are at liberty to walk in your freedom or suppose that this freedom is to be granted by another human being. Why must we take direction from people claiming to know what is best for us? Who better to determine my path than me? I am to abide by laws created by a person who has never sat down with me to discuss these laws. How can one possibly know that this particular law is what is needed to correct a wrong? More often than not, the thing that is needed in order to correct an issue has nothing to do with law and everything to do with humanity. We must supply a need; A need that has nothing to do with law or constraint. Basic human needs must be supplied to all humans. If we express our needs outward then the laws of attraction dictate that this is what will be returned. However, we ignore our spiritual impulse and place limitations on our thinking where the government becomes our cap and the media our regulator of information.

Wait...What?

Now see...
this shit here ain't what I came for
Got simple hood bitches at my door
Playing team petty
Shit makes my ass sore
You got ya jump off
Skipping her happy yamp ass
All up in my inbox
attempting to foxtrot
And I just wanna stomp
You wanna verbal romp
And I wanna molly wop
Got your mouth spilling shit
In my direction
When we share no affection
Betta holla at who you think yo man is
Instead of minding my biz
Truth is
You can't change me
Or my direction
And upon further reflection
The source of your issue
Does not spell T'challa
So don't come holla
Check your heart condition
By that man you missing
Got you all riled up and
Wondering who he kissing
Meditating on what you do not have
Girl don't make me laugh
Spring clean your situation
Stop chasing ass you think he sniffing
For you find your face with piss in it

Shedding of the fallacy

we hold on tight
plastered and paper machete`
Glued and sealed when it should be repealed
painted then decorated
And hated
Naked but not bearing truth
budding trees yet producing no fruit
just words shaped into experiences and tempting
to tell tales
with epic fails
Straw arms holding up imagery
Concrete density and always defining me
Slick words
Lose my grip
Slipping salacious phraseology
From root to tip

Bye

Just leave me
Allow me to sit
Crossed legs
Across from my reflection
poised and in duress
Though facial expression does not confess
There is an internal election
Between my mind and my heart
My heart won!
I will be saying
NO
To you
And yes
To the things I want done

Why is it you can proposition me for my time
But never ask me if everything is fine
Or bring me a bottle of wine (which rests next to your beer, dear)
Old English but no gentlemanly gestures here
Ignoring my requests and
Never one to bequeath
Hands always within my arms reach
Remembering my unquestioned
willingness to assist
You will find
I am dating 'NO' now
So 'ME' you will have to miss

Damn!

Slipped up and shared what you shouldn't
Wanted to take it back but you couldn't
Had a bitch hot like fire
Off a notification
Wanted to put your ass
On a pussy vacation
But I like you too damn much
And love your such and such
So I flipped out just a touch
Not nearly as colorful as I wanted to be
Had curse words flowing like a damn tsunami
Fucked up on some mo betta shit
Had me screaming like Kelis
Mouth wide and my head thrown back
Why did you have to mess up like that?
Don't share those things that you share with me
Showing another woman
What makes me sexually intrigued
Turning us both on
Is turning me off
Stirring her love and making me scoff
So many times I hear my heart say
Fuck this shit and just walk away
But you got my soul in this bitch
So, on your love I can't quit
I knew what it was when we first got started
Im gone act like your brain just farted
And you half-way retarded
Though passive aggressive and very accepting
I can go light to dark
And take your soul on a journey
Your heart won't return from
So let me make a suggestion

Don't regret what you already had listed
Number two can be number one
And you will forever miss it
Have you thinking you legit
As you stand in a pit
With depths like dante
Changing levels on you
Like an escalator to heaven
Or hell for that matter
Don't give me no pass
Cause you being an ass
Falling in and out of love
Can happen real fast
That one little thing you continue to neglect
Can have another muthafucka
Kissing my neck

Thinking of you

You run through thoughts
Bare chest at best
Dust
Kicked up past kneecaps
Running through
To
From
Coming undone
And reaching for another
Hands outstretched
Fingertips grazing molecules
Shifting components
Proponents to this love
Head tilted
Contemplating
Face kissed by sun's rays

Pen & No Paper

Why do we share
Lifting up the insufficient
like it wasn't faulty to start
It's not that I don't have heart
but this love is art, is bull
sometimes that shit is like getting teeth pulled.

Love Fucking Hurts

can't have what you want
what you have
doesn't give you the feeling you need
don't want to mind fuck yourself into believing
what you have is enough
blindly wrapped up in other folk's feelings just to drop the unhappy
besides,
your happy
is too far away
no one to share honest feelings with, other than this page
i wanna cry...for a while
and eat ice cream
i need a moment
because I miss my love

Just Grow!

You so progressive
That you
NOT
Progressing
You so aggressive
That you
Keep
Digressing
Stop serving liquid lips
Dripping ideologies & pseudo biographies of what you wish your life could
be but you too lazy to put the work in for
So upset that success takes work
You walking around being a jerk
In need of help
But you burned your bridges
A bleeding heart that can't get stitches
Coveting my riches
While you sit on your britches
Leave your pity party
Start an evolution revolution and evolve from a state of being
To a state of living
Stop talking
Start doing
It is your future you need to be pursuing
Not the defamation of me
Cause
I'm gone be alright!

Scratch & Smoke (Blues)

Small rooms
encompassing emotion
hazy silhouettes belly dancing and climbing to ceiling
while sending sound down
To drown
In short glasses

Scattered

Scattered like tattered dress
Lace fringes blowing in the wind
Billowing over dusty boot sleuth
Happened upon it all
Innocently saw it fall
Ordered away
as if sound
Did not paint pictures

Random

Nostalgia is an FB drug.
Giving people the illusion
they can make amends
when their time
has
passed

On locing Up

Nobody likes that part
The part you can't cover up
Those pieces that will not allow you
To neatly tuck them away
You must be exposed
Vulnerable
Open to yourself
We spend so much time putting on
That we forget how to take off
So we run from it
Try to give it other names
Trick us into perceiving it
As something other than what it is
No matter how you paint the phrase
You may not eliminate the days
Where you are naked
Open your arms
Lean your head back
And accept
The warmth and beauty
Of the ugly phase

Open the door (to the 9)

Did not want to
The thought of it all
Took my heart places
My hands could not respond quick enough to
All the hurt, in my view
Did not want external sources
Describing my history to me
Telling me what to be
And what I'm not seeing
Did not want to hear not one prayer
Or forgiving phrase
I was not feeling forgiving
I was feeling sadistic
Mind weaving endings
That would make you unfurl
Acts so very torturous
I don't even put them on paper
for fear my visions
Would come to be
So I calm me
And smirk

Did not want to delve into any article
That would leave my face wet
As militancy is replaced by the fact
that
I too
Am a granddaughter

How often we make it our business to acknowledge visitors
Especially when they have crossed some barrier to seek us out
We call them in our prayers
Mistaking close proximity with shared vision

We praying so much that we never listen

I didn't want to talk about how much I love that little building
Creaking wood floors
Comfort like your grandmother's house
A place where whatever you needed was provided
Topped with hugs and kisses
And pie or pound cake
Silence cracked open by the laughter of robust men
With baritone voices
And beautiful smiles
All the while
Their silver hair like halos
Everybody knows Deac!

Ruffled dress
Fresh hot comb press
And the raspy voice of an elder
Giving instruction
And lots of loving
Then

Nothing.

Nine
The number of my birth month
contained in my birthday
Nine lives
but I'm not talking 'bout no cats
NINE.
A number so much a part of me
been writing it all my life
Adding to and taking away
Nine, Nine, Nine,
Nine

Nine times I read that line
Hearing the nine made me want my 9
But now is not the time
No matter how quiet the room becomes
Or how much I want my guns
No matter how much I fall astray
Whether I do or don't pray
the doors of the church will always be open
with love and forgiveness as doormen
The Holy Ghost is your usher
Guiding you into His presence
where grace is in abundance
I am not your church
But there is a place
Where the door will always be open

You don't wanna war with us

You keep talking like you ready
all amped up and egging us on
We keep our head bowed
Resisting
Resisting
but still we are listening
I hear the undertones in your speech
fear is there also
Forever embedded in your hatred for me
But hate don't stop me from being
And what you not seeing is
Survival of the fittest is the rule of thumb
You must be dumb thinking you wanna come for us
Every piece of conniving strategy, plot derail
All your shit fail
And where you don't fail – you shift
Leaving the strongest to rise out the rift
Each level more powerful than the last
A cleverly designed bloodline
That you weren't even paying attention to
Helping us when you thought you were just helping you
You make your war stories and carefully craft media outputs
Laced with manipulated bullshit
Not realizing that the process exercised creative thinking
Learned to be quiet
Less talking, more thinking

You don't wanna come for us
the energy of our ancestors recycles and disperses
Its levels son
Once passed on they are quickly absorbed into the diaspora
Swelling our core
Expanding our reach

Boundaries breached
Drummers beating out strategies
Directly to our hearts
The diaspora responds in kind
And our souls sit and meditate
While you act a fool all around us
Attempt to understand our silence
We sit
Crossed legs
Eye cleansed
Meditating on the low hum
Like the Maasai
Soft and low
Should the volume increase
A beat felt in the soul
calling and connecting all of the colors of the continent
beneath a red, black and green flag
Fist up
There will be no regard for anything
No uniform, no edifice no social structure or construct of any form
There will no longer be a norm
This will not be a traditional fight
Cause
We fight dirty
After all......we learned from the best
You come for us
And we determine that it is time (yes, we make that decision)
Then everything must end
It must all be done away with
so we can start anew

You don't wanna war with us
we don't play to win
We plan to live
Remember?

Survival of the fittest

You don't want to war with us

Should we say we don't give a fuck

It's a wrap black

Been waiting all our lives to clap back

Think

Before you blink

And all this shit you know

Will be reduced to ink

Should we decide to allow your stories to be told

You don't want us cold

You bold

But this type of hatred is centuries old

Laced with juju and the anger of gods denied

Once turned on

It will not subside

So go on in the house

Play witcha lil friends

Cause you really don't want this world to end.

Big Bones & Undertones

You see her and think
why she so big
what she holding?
I'll answer cause
you can't see
you got that eye dirty
Her throne be generations of possibilities
You figga wide hips and hard nips
Be about you
naw, that's your flaw
perched on the yoni-verse is the enemy's curse
a premonition of unraveling's
an ending to all the fallacies

Fragrance

You smell of good cologne
and mixed berry candles
the faint hint of the finest cannabis
you smell like the birth of me
1974
Soul music and velvet pictures
reefa and afros
and the debris left by the 60s
Brown skin and that Jamaica poster
That made us all want to see the island
Your aroma is laced with black fists
Panther organizational structure
And the astuteness of Malcom X
You smell of black power
And the sexy aggression of black men
That makes the world cower
Black love incense
Dancing in an ebony sunrise
Madagascar in your eyes
A roar in your throat
Mighty and true
I smell the essence of man
A royal King
That is you

Love's Respite

I love you,
But I love me too
That means I'll do anything for you
Except not love myself
So when you put me on a shelf
Recognize, I am self cleaning
Self absorbed
And self polishing
You have positioned me to be seen
In my best light
That, is love's respite

Discharged

Police said, when you discharge your firearm
you are responsible for where the bullet goes

He was talking about celebratory gunfire
But I am talking about eating your words

Dead Seeds

I have no desire for death to swim in my pools
no urge to incubate her weariness
Or nurture her darkness
Or feed her bosom
Her health is no longer a concern of mine
We use to dine
Thought she was fine
Until we were alone
And realized her mind did not do what her body did
Did not billow amongst the breeze
Did not bring love to its knees

Falling

You are my first thought in the morning
And my last thought at night
Didn't think it would be right
But having you on my mind like this
Will have you on my mind all the time
Wanting you to be mine
Exclusively
Excluding all the b.s. and extracurricular mess
What we all want is to be important to someone
Important enough to be thought about all the time
I don't have to ask you if I'm on your mind
You always on my phone
Never leaving me alone
Witcha big ass head!
But that's what I want
Never to be left alone
When seeing you in my phone
Leads to seeing you seated next to me
Awake or sleeping
Silent or speaking
Yet always in my presence
In some kind of way
That's how you build love
Each day
And that's how you find your way
On a path to my heart
Journeying to my soul
Becoming a permanent part of me.

Last man

Didn't know I could feel this
Each day passed away
Yet never revealed this
Truths hidden away
In the caverns of my heart
With remnants on my skin
Like hieroglyphics
Humming stories when I run my hand against it
Heart beating out mating dances
Hips sway to the rhythm of you
I'm not just walking
I've identified rituals
Many tribes start love with a dance
Your words and tones
Inflections and expressions
Make my chest convulse
Hands flare up and back
Soul speaking on
Loving I lacked
And found
Now I dance around
In celebration of you
The circle is small
As it should be
This love need only you
And me
Anything else is decoration
This be my declaration
I have learned from my past
But this man that I love
Shall be my last

Transitional

You wanna know how I know the shift was real?
Because negroes came out the woodwork that same day
Same day the sun came out
So did the nostalgias
Pouring in my phone
Dripping manure from their mouths
Claiming it's from their heart
I see you choosy cats
Selective amnesia
Physical recollections
And sweaty homage
Funny how you don't see me
Till you can't see me
And by then you cain't see B!

A changing of the guard
Mind ruminating
Deleterious volitions
Seeking more because something's missing
I talk
But you don't listen

You Must Learn

What if the universe prepares you for love
But because your two eyes can't see depth
You miss the connection
So all those loves you recollect
Ones you can't seem to forget
Lessons on regret
Lessons on fully vetting
Lessons designed to unsnarl furled heart;
They are all pass fail
Your truest love wont set sail
Until you receive your degree
And black be blue
Six sigma is really nine
No belts for you
And when you can't figure out
Why you are where you are in relationships
Check who is joined to your hip
Is it love or lesson
lessons are designed to prepare you for what's real
But you got caught up in the temporary
And lost your permanent.
Much as I wanted my partner to teach me something
The idea of you teaching, scares me now
Feel like I'm losing ground
Afraid to change because society says
Don't change for no man
He should accept you as you are
But what if I'm fucked up
Got lies tucked up under my breast
And a lil too much lust on my breath
And not enough esteem to shine my light everyday
Too easy to let unworthy niggas prey
And what if he is helping me find my way

I want to resist

And he just persists

Unsettling my foundation

Can't even run game like I normally do

I'm sure if we look

there are lies we have convinced ourselves to be truths

Though uncouth

I'm letting him undo me

Reflex has me resisting arrest

I need to change more and fight less

Losing

Imagine being at the pinnacle of what you love
Nothing above you but God
And a chance to shine bright
like the sun you are
Caught up in two worlds
Duality
Decisions
Visions of what your future will be
And suddenly
The consequence of the smallest of decisions
Puts an incision in that vision

We Good

What are you doing to me?
I look at you and think
Girl go on somewhere and quit playing
You don't wanna be with him
I walk away
Till the next day
when
I look at you and think
I like them bow legs
And clean shave
Street niggas like nerdgirl elixir
Brew stirred and bewitched her
I step back and
Shake my head though
Snap out of it hoe!
Let that shit go!
So I push on
And you push in
Draped in sin but speaking blessings
We was just messing
Then messy turned chaos
Clear
You hear?
Questions that forced me to be real
And deal
And your hand be full house
And you ain't no louse
And we aint speaking spouse
But we good
And I'm good with that
You know
I like that you wanna take it slow

Fighting the fall

I can't give in
No matter how much I fall
Hands upon wall
Finger tips grab cliff
And
bleed
Bleed 'fore this love be freed
Got what I need
And I persist to resist
Why do I fight my heart about you?
What is my soul leary of?
If I give you love; will I feel
Pain
The pain of broken heart
Anxiety from anticipation of the end
Of something
I'm
Too afraid to begin, because
I don't want to see its end, so my
Hands are glued to the wall
Knees scrapped
Because my feet lost their footing
Heart rate up
but down is where I'm looking
Finger tips hold cliff
Sweat drips from brow to lip
Salty disposition
Compromising position

But...
I can't give in...
No matter how much
        your laughter brightens me

Frankness shocks me to reality
Or how much I sit on it (And I love my seat; Rock yo ass to sleep!)
No matter how bae subdued
Uprooted and old emotions booted
Debo'ed his chic and now she both....
Naw...she's yours
Every hair follicle and pore
I do...
But I won't say
Can't say
Not until I know without a doubt
That there is no turning back
Then I will be what you lack
what we share will be fair
And wherever you go
I will be there

Before anyone else

Gave me title first
Told me that's how you got me
I didn't notice initially
But I liked my title
And your swag
Had the whole block on notice
When that blue car come thru
That's you
It was your persistence and consistence
That got you through
I wasn't looking
And you wanted some cooking
So
Obedient as I am
Made that ass ham
 veggies, omelet, sandwiches
Chicken, & steak
I didn't want no break
I was happy to see you eat
Happy to give you a seat
At the table.

www.ingramcontent.com/pod-product-compliance
Lightning Source LLC
Chambersburg PA
CBHW020907090426
42736CB00008B/530